SIMPLY SCIENCE

The Solar System

by Dana Meachen Rau

Content Adviser: Terrence E. Young Jr., M.Ed., M.L.S.,
Jefferson Parish (La.) Public Schools

Reading Adviser: Dr. Linda D. Labbo,
Department of Reading Education, College of Education,
The University of Georgia

COMPASS POINT BOOKS

Minneapolis, Minnesota

Compass Point Books
3722 West 50th Street, #115
Minneapolis, MN 55410

Visit Compass Point Books on the Internet at *www.compasspointbooks.com* or e-mail your
request to *custserv@compasspointbooks.com*

Photographs ©:
NASA, cover; Visuals Unlimited/Gary W. Carter, 4; Photo Network/Douglas Pulsipher, 5; NASA, 7; Index Stock Imagery, 8;
E.O. Hoppe/Corbis, 10; Corbis, 11; NASA, 12, 14, 15 far left; Astronomical Society of the Pacific, 15 middle left, 15 middle right,
15 far right; NASA, 16 top far left, 16 top middle left, 16 top middle right, 16 top far right, 16 bottom; Roger Ressmeyer/Corbis,
18; Astronomical Society of the Pacific, 19, 21; NASA, 22, 23, 24, 25; Corbis, 26; Astronomical Society of the Pacific, 27, 28;
NASA 29.

Editors: E. Russell Primm, Emily J. Dolbear, and Melissa Stewart
Photo Researcher: Svetlana Zhurkina
Photo Selector: Dawn Friedman
Design: Bradfordesign, Inc.

Library of Congress Cataloging-in-Publication Data

Rau, Dana Meachen, 1971–
  The solar system / by Dana Meachen Rau.
    p. cm.— (Simply science)
  Includes bibliographical references and index.
  Summary: Briefly describes the characteristics of the sun, planets, moons, asteroids, and comets
of our solar system.
    ISBN 0-7565-0036-2 (hardcover : lib. bdg.)
    1. Solar system—Juvenile literature. [1. Solar system.] I. Title. II. Simply science
(Minneapolis, Minn.)
  QB501.3 .R43 2000
  523.2—dc21   00-008560

Table of Contents

What Is a Solar System?

Look up at the sky during the day.
Do you see the Sun? The Sun is a star.
Now look up at the sky at night.
Do you see many little specks of light?
Those are stars too. There are millions
and millions of stars scattered through-
out the universe. Some are larger
and brighter than
others. The Sun is a
small star. It looks
big and bright to
us because it is the
closest star
to Earth.

The sun setting over
the ocean

Stars at night

The Sun is very important to people on Earth. It gives us light and heat. The Sun is also important because it is the center of our **solar system**. Our solar system is the group of **planets** (including Earth) that **orbit**, or move around, the Sun along with many **moons**, **asteroids**, **meteoroids**, and **comets**.

Planets orbit the sun. ▶

Learning About Space

How do we learn about space? For thousands of years, people have looked up into the sky. At first, they believed that the Sun and all the planets orbited Earth. Then, about 400 years ago, a scientist named Nicolaus Copernicus said he believed that the Sun was the center of the solar system. He said that the planets orbit the sun in oval-shaped paths.

It took a long time for people to find out that Nicolaus Copernicus was right. Before they could get proof, they needed to look at the planets through

Nicolaus Copernicus believed that the sun, not Earth, was the center of our solar system.

telescopes. Telescopes made the Moon and planets seem closer, but some people wanted to get much closer. They wanted to visit these far-off places.

In the 1950s, scientists started to send machines into space. Some of these spacecraft flew by the planets and took close-up pictures.

In 1969, a spacecraft

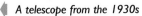 A telescope from the 1930s

Astronaut Buzz Aldrin on the moon

named *Apollo 11* carried the first people to the Moon. Spacecraft have helped us learn a lot about the solar system.

The Sun

How big is big? Some dogs are big. Buildings are big. Countries are big. Earth is big. But the Sun is so big that more than one million Earths could fit inside it.

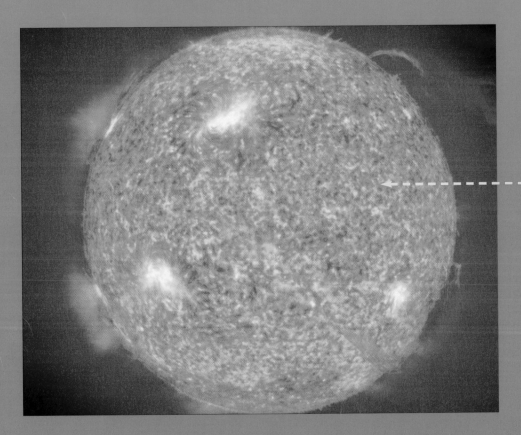

The Sun is also very hot and active. The temperature at the center of the Sun is 27 million degrees Fahrenheit (15 million degrees Celsius). Hot, fiery storms shoot out of its surface.

To people on Earth, it seems as if the Sun is moving. The Sun rises and sets every day. Even on cloudy days, the Sun still crosses the sky. We see the Sun in the east in the morning. By late after-noon, the Sun has moved to the west.

The Sun does not really move, but Earth does. Earth orbits the Sun, and it spins like a top. When one side of Earth spins to face the Sun, it is nighttime on the other side of the world.

◀ Fire storms, called eruptions,
shoot out from the sun.

The Planets

Nine planets orbit the Sun. The planet closest to the Sun is Mercury. Then come Venus, Earth, Mars, Jupiter, Saturn, Uranus, Neptune, and Pluto.

The orbits of the planets in our solar system and their size in relation to the sun

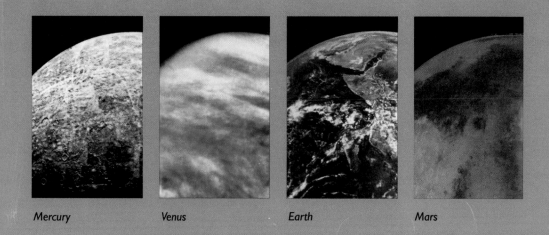

Mercury   Venus   Earth   Mars

The first four planets, Mercury, Venus, Earth, and Mars, are called the inner planets or rocky planets. They have solid, rocky surfaces. The next five planets, Jupiter, Saturn, Uranus, Neptune, and Pluto, are called the outer planets or gas planets.

All of the outer planets, except Pluto, are made up mostly of gases and have rings orbiting them. Rings are pieces of rock, ice, and dust circling around a planet. Saturn has the most rings.

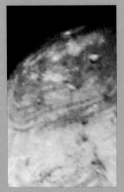

Saturn

Uranus

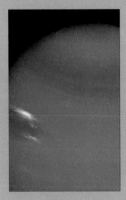

Neptune

Pluto and its moon
Charon

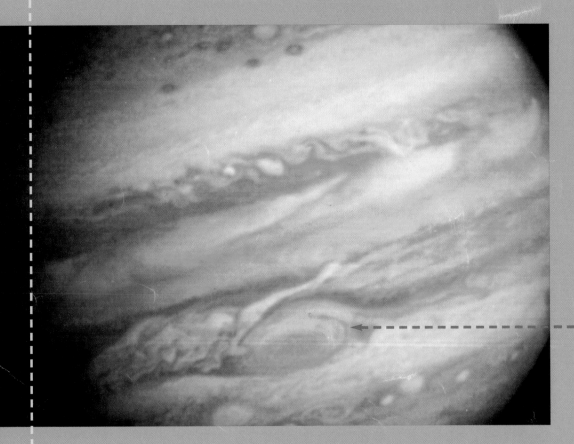

Pluto is very different from the other planets. It is frozen, dark, and made of rock and ice.

Pluto is the smallest planet in the solar system. Jupiter is the largest. Scientists are always searching for even more planets orbiting the Sun.

As far as we know, Earth is the only planet that has living things. It is at just the right distance from the Sun for plants and animals to grow and live.

◀ *Jupiter showing Great Red Spot*

Moons

Many of the planets have moons. Moons orbit around the planets just like the planets orbit around the Sun.

The surface of Earth's Moon is covered with craters, or holes. Many spacecraft have been sent to the Moon to study it. Some of the astronauts who landed on the Moon brought back rocks for scientists to study.

Scientists study a moon rock.

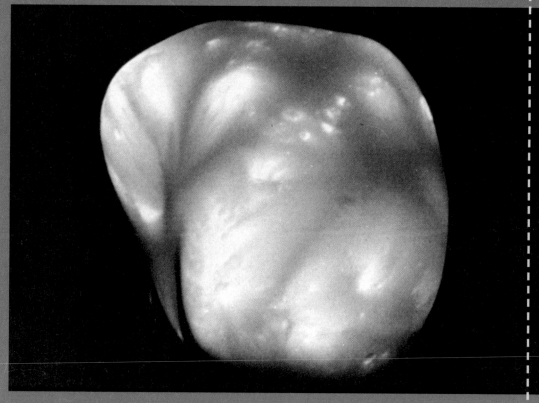

Deimos, a moon of Mars

The Moon looks bright to us, but it doesn't give off light. The Moon's light comes from the Sun. When you look at the Moon, you see light reflected off the Sun. Sometimes you can even see the Moon during the day.

Have you ever noticed that the Moon looks a little bit different every night? One night, the Moon is bright and full. A week later, you can only see half of the Moon. As the Moon moves around Earth, different amounts of sunlight are reflected off the surface of the Moon.

You are probably asleep when the Moon sets. But if you watched it all night, you would see that it moves across the sky just like the Sun. It rises in the east and sets in the west. That is because Earth is always spinning.

Only one other inner planet has moons. Mars has two moons—Deimos and Phobos. The other moons in the solar system circle the outer planets.

Jupiter has sixteen moons. Four of them are large—Io, Europa, Ganymede, and Callisto. Ganymede is the largest moon in the solar system.

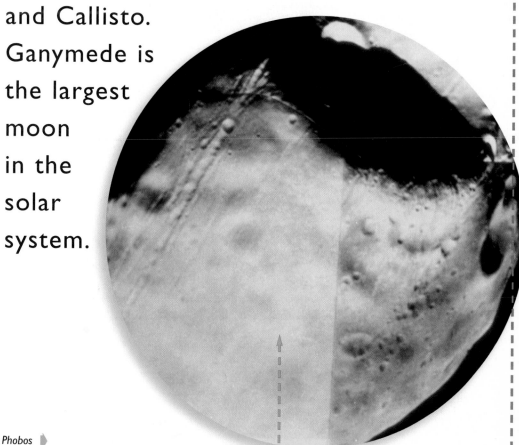

Phobos ▶

It is even larger than the planet Mercury. Saturn has eighteen moons. One of them is Titan, the second-largest moon in the solar system.

Scientists believe that Uranus may have as many as twenty-one moons, but only seven- teen have been named.

Jupiter with its moon
Ganymede

Saturn ▶

The innermost moon is named Cordelia. It is one of the smallest moons in the solar system. Titania is the largest moon of Uranus.

Neptune has at least eight moons. Neptune's largest moon Triton is thought to be the coldest place in the solar system.

Pluto has one moon, named Charon. Charon is about one-half the size of pluto itself.

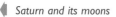 *Saturn and its moons*

Triton, Neptune's largest moon ▶

Asteroids and Comets

Asteroids are pieces of rock and metal that orbit the Sun. Most of them are located in an asteroid belt that lies between the orbits of Mars and Jupiter.

Sometimes an asteroid breaks free from its orbit. Then it is called a meteoroid. Meteoroids may hit planets or moons. When a meteoroid hits a planet or moon, it is called a **meteorite**. You can see the many craters created when meteorites hit our own Moon.

Asteroid 243 Ida is thirty-five miles long and has its own moon.

Craters on Earth's moon

Comets are made of frozen ice and dust. Most comets have very large orbits. They come from an area of the solar system that is as far away as Pluto. When a comet gets close to the Sun, some of its icy center melts. The "tail" you see behind a comet is made of the gases and dust that fall away from a comet when it melts.

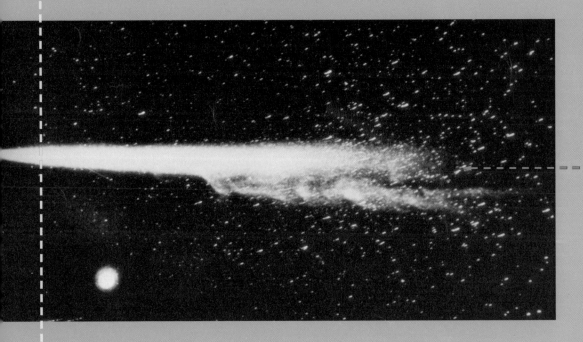

More Discoveries

Are there other solar systems as big as ours? Scientists don't think there are other stars with such a large system of planets and other objects orbiting around them. Since 1995, however, scientists have discovered almost twenty planets orbiting other stars.

Many people think there are many solar systems in space. They may be too far away for our telescopes and space-craft to find, but perhaps we will discover them someday. We may even discover another planet like Earth.

Comet Halley

The Hubble Space Telescope took pictures of thousands of galaxies that had never been seen before.

Glossary

asteroids—large chunks of rock or metal that orbit the Sun

comets—objects made of frozen gas and dust that orbit the Sun

meteorite—a chunk of rock or metal that has hit a planet or moon

meteoroids—chunks of rock or metal floating in the solar system

moons—objects that orbit around a planet

orbit—to move around

planets—the nine large objects that orbit the Sun

solar system—a group of planets and other objects that orbit a star, such as our Sun

telescopes—tools that make faraway objects seem closer

Did You Know?

- The solar system is about 4.6 billion years old.

- If Earth were the size of a grape, Jupiter would be the size of a grapefruit and the Sun would be the size of a 6-foot (1.8-m)-tall beach ball.

- Scientists have identified almost 900 comets and more than 100,000 asteroids.

- There are sixty-seven known moons in the solar system. Two of them orbit asteroids.

Want to Know More?

At the Library

Branley, Franklyn Mansfield. *The Sun and the Solar System*. New York: Twenty-First Century Books, 1996.

Branley, Franklyn Mansfield. *The Planets in Our Solar System*. New York: Harper Collins Publishers, 1998.

Levy, David H. *Stars & Planets*. Alexandria, Va.: Time-Life Books, 1996.

Sipiera, Paul P. *The Solar System*. Danbury, Conn.: Children's Press, 1997.

On the Web

Solar System Simulator

http://space.jpl.nasa.gov/

For full-color graphic views of the solar system

Welcome to the Planets

http://pds.jpl.nasa.gov/planets/

For images and information from NASA's planetary-exploration program

Through the Mail

Jet Propulsion Laboratory

4800 Oak Grove Drive

Pasadena, CA 91109

For information about NASA's planetary missions

On the Road

Kennedy Space Center

SR 405

Cape Canaveral, FL 32899

321/452-2121

To learn about space and see rockets and spacecraft that carried astronauts to the Moon

Index

About the Author

Ever since Dana Meachen Rau can remember, she has loved to write. A graduate of Trinity College in Hartford, Connecticut, Rau works as a children's book editor and illustrator and has authored many books for children, including biographies, non-fiction, early readers, and historical fiction. When Rau is not writing, she is watching the stars with her husband, Chris, and son, Charlie, in Farmington, Connecticut.